Ancient Ephesus: The History and Legacy of One of Antiquity's Cities

By Charles River Editors

Benh Song's picture of the Library of Celsus in Ephesus

About Charles River Editors

Charles River Editors provides superior editing and original writing services across the digital publishing industry, with the expertise to create digital content for publishers across a vast range of subject matter. In addition to providing original digital content for third party publishers, we also republish civilization's greatest literary works, bringing them to new generations of readers via ebooks.

Sign up here to receive updates about free books as we publish them, and visit Our Kindle Author Page to browse today's free promotions and our most recently published Kindle titles.

Introduction

A picture of the ruins of the Bath of Varius in Ephesus

Ephesus

"We shall never know what magnificence is, until this imperial city is laid bare to the sun." - Mark Twain

"I have set eyes on the wall of lofty Babylon on which is a road for chariots, and the statue of Zeus by the Alpheus, and the hanging gardens, and the colossus of the Sun, and the huge labour of the high pyramids, and the vast tomb of Mausolus; but when I saw the house of Artemis that mounted to the clouds, those other marvels lost their brilliancy, and I said, 'Lo, apart from Olympus, the Sun never looked on aught so grand.'" - Antipater

Although it is no longer quite as well remembered as it was thousands of years ago, one of the most important cities in the ancient world was Ephesus, a city that dates back nearly 3,000 years and can lay claim to the Temple of Artemis, one of the Seven Wonders of the Ancient World. Moreover, while Sparta and Athens were often the centers of power in ancient Greece, Ephesus, located in present-day Turkey on the coast of Ionia, was an instrumental part of the Ionian League, which wielded power for a substantial period of time before the Classical Era.

Thanks to its strategic location, Ephesus was an important city no matter who was in control of the region. In fact, while many of its most famous buildings were completed by 500 BCE, the city flourished after it became part of Rome's domains, and the Romans respected the culture so much that they continued letting Ephesus use original coins. In turn, as the Western Roman Empire dissolved and the Eastern Roman Empire and Byzantine Empire maintained control in the area, Ephesus became an important religious center. In addition to a shrine inspired by the Virgin Mary, Ephesus was mentioned repeatedly in the Bible, including in the New Testament's Revelations, and St. Paul even wrote some of the epistles in Ephesus.

Ironically, and unfortunately, it was Ephesus' role as an important place for early Christians that ensured the final destruction of its most famous feature: the Temple of Artemis. One of the oldest of the Wonders, construction began under King Croesus around 541 BCE, and it was constructed of marble in place of a previous structure that had been destroyed by a flood. The 3rd century Hellenic African scholar Callimachus of Cyrene believed the older structure had been built by the Amazons, but the original Temple of Artemis actually dated back to the late Greek Bronze Age around 1000 BCE. It may have been the first columned temple of its kind, but the site was not considered a Wonder of the World until after Croesus' version was built.

Unlike the other wonders, the enormous temple had two lives and two deaths. The first time it was destroyed, an arsonist named Herostratus burned it down in 358 BCE in the (apparently accurate) belief that such destruction would make him famous. The city's inhabitants promptly executed him and made it illegal to mention his name thereafter, but the gossipy 4th century Greek historian Theopompus recorded the deed in his book, *The Hellenics*, anyway. Oddly enough, ancient historians noted that the burning coincided with the birth of Alexander the Great, and Plutarch credits the destruction of the temple with the fact that Artemis was too preoccupied with Alexander's birth to save her own temple.

A lot of information about the history of the Temple of Artemis remains unknown. It was built three times in all before its final destruction by the Goths in 262 CE, but the site's history thereafter is unclear before its rediscovery in 1869. It may have been repaired after the 3rd century CE, but this did not prevent it from being pillaged for building materials to construct Christian buildings in Constantinople a couple of centuries later. Early Christians resented the temple because of its cult and following, and stories in the New Testament survive of early saints praying to exorcise it, causing physical destruction, or being forbidden from entering the city due to citizens' fears of damage to the temple. These tales may reflect real-life instances of attempted arson or vandalism.

Ancient Ephesus: The History and Legacy of One of Antiquity's Greatest Cities looks at the influential city and the way it flourished for centuries. Along with pictures depicting important people, places, and events, you will learn about Ephesus like never before.

Ancient Ephesus: The History and Legacy of One of Antiquity's Greatest Cities

About Charles River Editors

Introduction

   Chapter 1: Legendary Beginnings

   Chapter 2: The Persian Wars

   Chapter 3: The Peloponnesian War

   Chapter 4: Roman Ephesus

   Chapter 5: Byzantine Ephesus

   Online Resources

   Bibliography

Chapter 1: Legendary Beginnings

An aerial view of the ruins

With a history that extends all the way back to the Neolithic Age, Ephesus is truly an ancient city. Archaeologists working on the settlement mounds (höyuk) near Ephesus have found that the area was inhabited by 6000 BCE, and some ancient legends claimed that Ephesus was first settled by the Amazons, the legendary tribe of female warriors. At some point long before the Trojan War, the Amazons were said to have founded a sanctuary to their nature goddess Cybele somewhere in the hills surrounding the nearby Mount Solmissus. Here they placed a statue of the goddess, girded in a ceremonial multi-breasted dress and a turret-crown, and on the coast just below Ephesus lay the sacred grove of Ortygia, the primitive seat of this nature goddess.

According to Homer, these Amazons joined the side of the Phrygian King Priam against Menelaus and his Achaean troops during the Trojan War, and excavations of the area around Ephesus have revealed the remains of an early Bronze Age settlement at Ayasuluk Hill that an increasing number of scholars believe may well have been the elusive city known to the ancients as Troy. According to the Hittites, this settlement—known to them as Apasa—was the capital of the Kingdom of Arzawa, an independent state believed to be located in Western or Southern Anatolia.

The Trojans lost to the Achaeans, and the result ushered in an era of Mycenaean rule in the Phrygian region. This era was also known as the period of Mycenaean Expansion, as this was the point at which the Achaeans (Greeks) first began to settle in Asia Minor. 14th century Hittite sources mention that the city of Apasa was then ruled by the Ahhiyawanas, which is most likely a Hittite rendering of "Achaean." Of course, Ephesus was no exception, and some excavations have unearthed a Mycenaean era (1500–1400 BCE) burial ground.

At some point between 1200 and 1150 BCE, Mycenaean rule of Ephesus and the surrounding areas was brought to an end by the Dorians,[1] who took up a series of invasions against Mycenaean Greece. Thereafter, the palaces and cities of the Mycenaeans were either abandoned or destroyed, and the entire Mycenaean region plummeted into the Greek Dark Age. During this period, the inhabitants of the Hellenic mainland lost almost all contact with foreign nations, cultural progress slowed to a grinding halt (and indeed even began to reverse), and the region's written language, Linear B, was forgotten entirely.

In the years immediately following the Dorian invasions (1130–1000 BCE), the Dorians began to migrate south to Greece, displacing those who inhabited the mainland. A number of these Greeks re-established themselves along the southwestern and western shores of Ionia over the course of several centuries, most likely continuing to do so until around the 7th century BCE. Gradually, however, the Greeks came to colonize the coasts of Asia Minor, thereby inheriting the city they would soon call Ephesus.

In the Greek tradition, the mythological foundation of Ephesus dates back to the 10th century. According to the Greeks, the founder of Ephesus was Androcles, a prince of Athens who was forced to flee the city upon the death of his father, King Cadros. Before his journey, Androcles had visited the oracle to Apollo at Delphi, and the oracle, who always spoke cryptically, informed Androcles that a fish and a boar would show him the way to the site of his city.[2] The meaning of the oracle's words became clear when Androcles and his companions were roasting fish over an open fire. Suddenly, a fish flew from the pan into the dry brush nearby. The sparks from the fire ignited the brush, causing a boar to come running out in order to escape the blaze. Recalling the oracle's prophecy, Androcles leapt up and gave chase to the boar. The location in which he slayed this boar—the base of Mount Koressos—became the site on which he founded the city of Ephesus.

According to this tradition, it was Androcles who drove most of the Lelegians and Carians from the city of Ephesus and subsequently divided the residents of Ephesus into three tribes. The

---

[1] An Indo-European race originating from the Balkans. It was claimed that the Dorians were the descendants of the demigod hero Heracles.
[2] In another rendering of this myth, Androcles was sent to seek new land for the settlement of the increasingly excessive population of mainland Greece. When Androcles and his Athenian companions set out on their journey to colonize the region of Ionia, the Muses "in the form of bees guided their fleets, for they rejoiced in Ionia because the waters of Meles are sweeter than the waters of Cephisus and Olmeius." To commemorate these bee-guides, the Ephesians are known to have minted silver coins embossed with the image of a bee.

first tribe was the Ephesis, the peoples who were the true natives of Ephesus. The colonists from Athens were deemed Eumonumoi, and colonists having hailed from all other regions of Greece were the Bembinaeans. To govern the affairs of his new city and its tribes, Androcles established a council and an assembly of the people. One of the first ordinances of this council was to grant immunity to all those who resided near the ancient sanctuary of Cybele. In accordance with the prophecy of a Delphic oracle, they also constructed temples to both Athena and Apollo.

With Ephesus thus founded, Androcles took to campaigning against Samos, a neighboring island. Androcles managed to successfully capture Samos and retain both it and its neighbors for the better part of a decade. Eventually, he and his Ephesian troops were able to altogether expel the Samians from their island by accusing Leogoras, the ruler of the island, and his people of conspiring against the rest of the Ionians. Androcles' Samian triumph was, however, relatively short-lived; not long after his expulsion from Samos, Leogoras erected a wall on the mainland that faced Samos. 10 years later, the Samians were able to cross back over to the island and reclaim their home. It was then the Ephesians' turn to be cast off the island.

Androcles did not fare better in his attempt to save the peoples of Priene from the savage Caarians. Although his troops were victorious, Androcles himself did not survive the campaign. His men took his body back to be interred at Ephesus, where he was immortalized in monuments, reliefs, friezes, and coins that depicted him killing the wild boar, fighting against the Samosians, or perishing at the hands of the Carians. For centuries, the Ephesians considered Androcles' descendants to be kings and therefore awarded them the privilege of sitting in the front seats at the games and wearing purple robs as a reminder of their royal descent.

By the beginning of the 8th century, the Cimmerians, a predatory nomadic tribe that had begun to feel pressured by the tribes of the Scythians, started targeting Ionia, and their commander, Lygdamis, had no intention of sparing the city of Ephesus. The city managed to survive, but its temple to Artemis sustained so much damage that the locals believed the offended goddess incited a terrible plague among the Cimmerians as they fled to Cilcia.

As Ephesus was recovering from the deadly plague it suffered during the first decade of the 6th century, its tyrant, Melas II, believed that it was best to enter into a non-aggression pact with Alyattes. The pact stipulated that Melas II was to be married to one of Alyattes' daughters, and the marriage produced a son, Pindar, who eventually succeeded Melas II as tyrant of Ephesus. Though Pindar was said to be stern and unyielding in the punishments he delivered to Ephesian citizens, he was a generally reasonable ruler who was willing to take whatever precautions were necessary in order to protect his city from being subdued by barbarians.

In 560, Alyattes bequeathed his Lydian empire to his son, Croesus, and in the first year of his reign, Croesus began to move against the Greeks in Ionia, making Ephesus his first target. From the ancient days of the Amazons, the temple to Artemis had been deemed inviolate, and with this in mind, Pindar was inspired to consecrate the city of Ephesus to the goddess, thereby extending its inviolability. In order to accomplish this dedication, the Ephesians used ropes to connect the city's gates and towers to the columns of Artemis' temple, and Pindar even sent an envoy of Ephesians to go before Croesus as suppliants. Upon hearing the pleas of these Ephesians, it is said that Croesus laughed and generally accepted the stratagem. Though he ordered Pindar to leave the city, Croesus allowed the Ephesians to retain their freedom unmolested, and since the Temple to Artemis had been severely damaged or perhaps even destroyed in his initial attack on Ephesus, Croesus himself ordered the construction of a new Temple to Artemis. Ground was broken in 540 BCE, and the construction would continue for the next several decades.

A 6th century coin depicting Croesus

An ancient amphora depicting Croesus

A model of the Temple of Artemis at Miniatürk Park in Istanbul, Turkey. Photo by Zee Prime

Croesus' temple was an enormous building for its time, being about 430 feet long and nearly 60 feet tall with 127 marble columns. It had a cedar ceiling and doors made of cypress. Dedicated to Artemis, the virgin Greek goddess of the hunt, who was later conflated with the Roman goddess Diana, Ephesus and its amazing temple were the center of the cult of Artemis throughout the Greek world, and the Ephesians considered her *their* goddess, resenting any claims by foreigners to her origins. This version of Artemis, in fact, predated Hellenic civilization, and she was noted for her fertility even more than her virginity.

Within the temple, the statue of Artemis was made of wood and kept covered by jewelry. It also either had many breasts, or was hung with eggs or bull testicles, depending on the source. Her image was carried through the streets during the Artemisia festival, much the way saints' images are carried through the streets on holy days in Catholic countries. The image is even described in the Book of Acts in the Bible as having fallen down from the sky. The festival was universal to the Greeks, not unlike the Olympics, though the Artemisia festival was intended to promote marriage rather than physical prowess, with young men and women seeking out spouses during it. The goddess was served by a number of priestesses, many of them slaves and/or virgins.

The Lady of Ephesus, 1st century CE (Ephesus Archaeological Museum)

Much more is known of the Temple of Artemis than of some other Wonders because its foundations have survived and have been excavated. It was the favorite Wonder of Antipater of Sidon, who recorded a kind of religious epiphany in his brief description of it. It also inspired many copies, both in the Classical and Neo-Classical period. The insistence on rebuilding it in a place prone to destructive floods indicates that the site was extremely important to the worshipers of Artemis' cult, though Roman historian Pliny the Elder suggested a more practical reason for the site. He claimed that the Temple was built on wetlands to avoid being destroyed by earthquakes. This does not explain the insistence on building there after destruction by so many floods, but it may explain the original decision to select the site. The Mediterranean basin, and Anatolia especially, is prone to violent earthquakes. Most of the Wonders suffered damage from quakes and some were even destroyed outright.

Drum from the base of a column from the 4th century rebuilding.

Another indication of the Temple and the site's local importance was that the Ephesians so resented the intrusions of Persian worship into the temple after the defeat of Croesus by Cyrus the Great that they politely refused Alexander's help and money in the 4th century to rebuild it. They may also have been motivated by the coincidence that Herostratus burned the building the same night that Alexander was born.

Regardless, the civic identity of Ephesus appears to have been tied up with the welfare of the Temple. Once it burned and was apparently abandoned, Ephesus would also fade in prestige.

The site of the Temple of Artemis today. Photo by Adam Carr

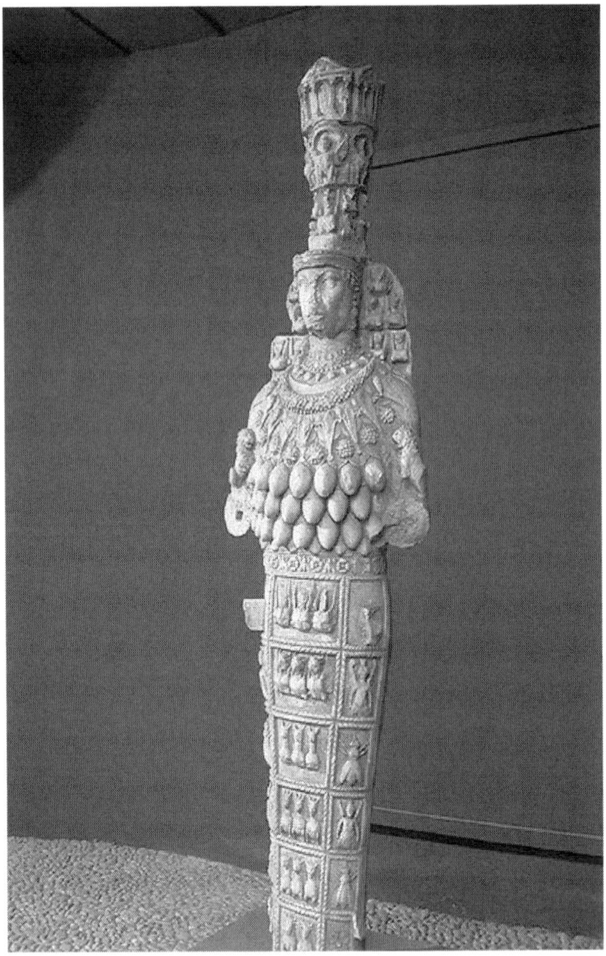

Pictures of statues of Artemis in Ephesus

Chapter 2: The Persian Wars

By the dawn of the 5th century, the Persians had replaced the Lydians as the dominant power in Asia Minor. The Persians frequently intruded in local affairs, levied heavy taxes, and conscripted the strongest of their subjects into the Persian army, and by 499, the Ionians had had enough. Histiaeus, a Milesian tyrant, called for revolt, and before long, the Ionian states were organized in an anti-Persian alliance. The Athenian democratic assembly, seeing the Ephesians as Androcles' descendants and "Ionian settlers," were quick to lend their support by sending 25 ships to join the Ionians assembled at Ephesus.

With the Athenians and their fellow Ionians, the Ephesians began to march up the Cayster Valley to Sardis. Attacking the Lydian stronghold, they annihilated the city and laid siege to its acropolis, but soon, the Persian troops came to the aid of the Lydian satrap, who happened to be the brother of Darius I. The Ionians had to beat a hasty retreat to Ephesus, where they were thoroughly routed. The Ionians thus defeated, the Athenians promptly withdrew their support, leaving the Ephesians to fend for themselves. Not long after the departure of the Athenians, the Ephesians, upon seeing Chian troops withdrawing from the Battle of Miletus, managed to muster their remaining forces and, having mistaken the Chians for the enemy, slew them.

A Persian relief depicting Darius I

The Ionians somehow managed to sustain their revolt for six years until 494, when it was crushed by the Persian general Mardonius. Two years later, Darius I sent Mardonius against Athens to retaliate since Athens had interfered in the Ionian Revolt, but the Persian navy was destroyed by violent winds off Mt. Athos. Darius I, undeterred, prepared for a second attack, and in 490, the Persian army, under the command of the generals Artaphernes II and Datis, crossed the Greek mainland and made for the plain of Marathon in Attica. There, they faced off against the Athenians, who had chosen Callimachus as their general. The Ephesian auxiliaries who had accompanied the Persian forces managed to escape to Callimachus' camp. The Ionian envoy was welcomed by their fellow Greeks, and several were sent back into the array in the hopes that they would be able to incite their fellow Ionians and turn them against the Persians. The battle was bloody, but in the end the Athenians were victorious, and the Persians retreated through Asia Minor.

When the Persian king Darius I died in 486, life in the Greek cities of Asia Minor changed little. Each city was permitted to retain some degree of autonomy at the hands of a tyrant ruler, so long as that ruler continued to pay tribute to the Persians through their Lydian satraps. Darius I was succeeded by his son, Xerxes I (reigned 485-465), who was preoccupied almost immediately with a Babylonian uprising and a minor secession attempt on the part of the Egyptians. However, once both of these issues had been sufficiently resolved, Xerxes turned his attention to the Greeks, whom the Persians had not yet managed to punish for their part in the Ionian Revolt.

A relief depicting Xerxes

Xerxes spent five years meticulously planning this third expedition against the Greek mainland, and in 480, the Persian forces finally began to move against Greece. After defeating the Spartan king Leonidas and his 300 men at Thermopylae in Thessaly, Xerxes and his elite Immortals ravaged the city of Athens. The Athenian navy, commanded by Eurybiades and Themistocles, withdrew to the coasts of Salamis, and when the Persian fleet attempted to follow them into the narrow channel that lay between Salamis and the mainland, the Greeks were ready for them and utterly defeated the Persian fleet.

Thus defeated, what remained of the Persian fleet retreated to Samos so that they would be able to keep an eye on Ionia and the other coastal cities of Asia Minor. At the same time, the Hellenic fleet, commanded by Leutychides and Xanthippus, set sail for Delos and met with several ambassadors from Samos, who encouraged them to consider liberating the Greeks in Asia. When the Persian admirals learned of this, they quickly withdrew from Samos and benched their ships a short distance from Miletus, but before long, they were pursued by Leutychides, the Ephesians, and the other Greeks of Asia Minor, whose hearts had been overcome with "an overwhelming desire for liberty."

Upon returning from his battles in Greece, Xerxes made a brief stop in Ephesus, where he picked up a few of his illegitimate sons he had left there with their guardian, the chief eunuch Hermotimus of Pedasa. Xerxes' sons and their guardian had been deposited in Ephesus by the Carian queen Artemesia of Halicarnassus, who had fought under Xerxes at Salamis. At Ephesus, Xerxes' sons had been granted protection at the Temple of Artemis, which was now nearing completion.

The Temple of Artemis provided protection to all those within its walls, but its immunity was not limited to people. All money deposited within the Temple of Artemis for safekeeping was also granted protection, though perhaps not surprisingly, deposits made to the Temple of Artemis at Ephesus were not necessarily immune to theft and mismanagement. Herodotus suggests that Ionia was not a secure place for the depositing of the wealth one had acquired, citing an unnamed depositor he had met who claimed that "Ionia is as ever a land of dangers, and in Ionia nowhere are the same men seen continuing in possession of wealth."

After Xerxes left Ephesus and returned home to Persia, Athens became the chief naval power in the Aegean region, and as the 3rd century moved into its third decade, Athens had become the defender of the Ionian city states and the Aegean islands. Though the Athenians had won a number of important battles, they had not yet won the Greco-Persian War, as the Persians' Phoenician fleet was still powerful and their large land force ensured control over the majority of Asia Minor and its eastern territories.

In 478–477, Athens created an anti-Persian alliance—the Delian League—in order to deal with the continued Persian threat. The Delian League (known also as the Confederacy of Delos) was comprised of the Athenians, the Hellespont, the Propontis, the Ionian maritime cities, and the majority of the Aegean islands, which meant the League formed a close, defensive ring around the Aegean Sea. The League's treasury was located on the central island of Delos in the Cyclades, which came to be the alliance's meeting point.

Since Athens was by far the richest and most powerful member of the Delian League, it quickly came to dominate the alliance, and Ephesus and the other members of the League soon found themselves bound to the whims of Athens, which did not hesitate to manipulate her allies for her own gain. Eventually, the Delian League came to be fraught with resentment, and Athens became outright oppressive to its fellow members. Before long, the League's treasury was moved from Delos to Athens, and at this point, Athens took it upon herself to strictly assess the League's member-cities and states, coercing each member to go beyond its means in order to contribute the requisite quota money.

In 467, the Cycladian island of Naxos revolted against the Delian League, and Thasos, an island located in the northern Aegean, followed suit in 465. Athens did not stand for these revolts; after a two year siege, Cimon, who commanded the League's fleet, retook Thasos.

At some point during this two year siege, a palace conspirator murdered Xerxes at Persepolis. Xerxes was succeeded by his son, Artaxerxes. Upon his ascent, Artaxerxes almost immediately began to experience setbacks in Asia Minor as Cimon managed a double victory over the Persian sea and land forces at the mouth of the Eurymedon River in Pamphylia.

Though the Greco-Persian War would not technically come to an end for almost two more decades, Cimon's victory effectively secured Athenian control of southern Asia Minor. In 449, Greece and Persia negotiated the so-called Peace of Callias, in which it was stipulated that Greek Ionia would be given independence and the Persians would henceforth refrain from bringing their fleet into the waters of the Aegean.

Chapter 3: The Peloponnesian War

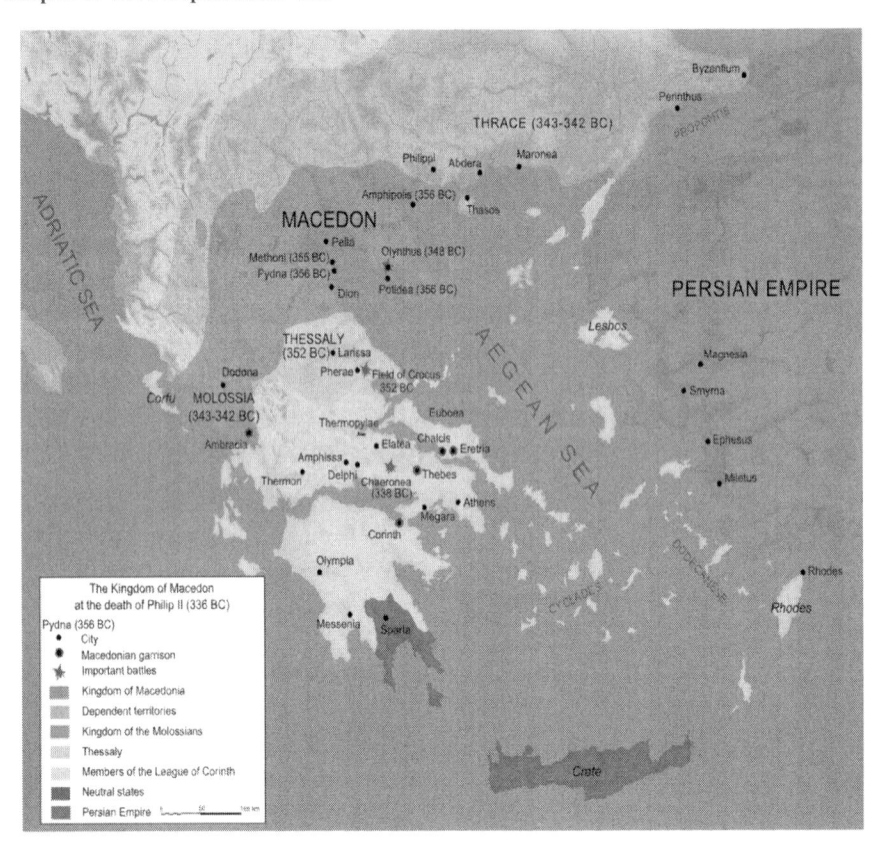

A map of the region in the 4th century

Ephesus' respite from war was, as usual, short-lived. In 431, the Peloponnesian War began when the Athenian statesman Pericles decided to interfere in a dispute between Sparta's ally Corinth and a rebellious colony of Corinth's called Cocrcyra, an island located in the Ionian Sea just off the coast of Epirus. Pericles allied himself with the rebels, and their combined naval force was effectively able to defeat the Corinthian fleet in the waters near the Sybota islands. Then, not quite one year later, the Athenian admiral Phormion laid siege to the Corinthian colony of Poteidaia in the Chalcice, and after two years, Poteidaia finally surrendered.

Pericles

With that, Corinth made an appeal to Sparta, which promptly declared war on Athens. The decade was characterized by a number of frequent and gory but inconclusive skirmishes between the two powers and their allies. Throughout the war there were shifting alliances and constant naval deployments. In order to protect the integrity of their territory, the Hellenic islands and city-states found themselves forced to ally and re-ally with whatever power was strongest or sometimes even just closest at the time. Each city-state was also obliged to provide conscripted auxiliary forces in order to assist its allies in the ongoing conflict.

Naturally, Ephesus was allied with its Athenian "defenders." Indeed, in one of his Socratic dialogues, Plato has Socrates ask the Ephesian rhapsode Ion why he would not want to be a general in the armed forces, to which Ion replied, "Why, Socrates, the reason is that my countrymen, the Ephesians, are the servants and soldiers of Athens and do not need a general, and you and Sparta are not likely to have me, for you think that you have enough generals of your own!"

424 saw the death of Artaxerxes I, as well as the assassination of two of his successors, Xerxes II and Sogdianus. After the assassination of Sogdianus, the throne passed to Darius II (423–405), who was nicknamed "the illegitimate." It was in this precipitous political climate that Sparta decided to sue for peace, but the resultant Peace of Nicias did not last long. The Athenian aristocrat Alcibiades, displaying an astonishing lack of forethought, entered Athens into an anti-Spartan alliance with the city-states Mantineia, Elis, and Argos. Agis II, the king of Sparta, was understandably offended and responded with aggression, and the Athenian alliance was promptly defeated in 418 at the Battle of Mantineia.

A bust of Alcibiades

In 415, Alcibiades doubled down on his poor political judgment by persuading Athens to dispatch a large force to the island of Sicily. Immediately before the force was set to depart, a group of young men went about the city defacing the faces of the Hermes statues that were ubiquitous in the city of Athens. Alcibiades was implicated in this wanton act of sacrilegious vandalism; however, he left for Sicily before any formal charges could be brought against him. Once his ship landed at Catana, however, an Athenian state trireme arrived to recall him to Athens on the formal charge of impiety. Alcibiades fled to Cyllene, where he remained until he received summons to Sparta from the Spartans themselves, who promised him safe-conduct. In return, Alcibiades provided the Syracusans—by then hard-pressed by the Athenian fleet—with immediate aid. In 413, the Syracusians were able to decisively defeat the Athenians in the harbor of Syracuse. Thereafter, the Sicilian fleet played a significant role in the war; they defended the city of Miletus against its seemingly inevitable capture by the Athenians and they came to the aid of Ephesus when it was assailed by an Athenian commander named Thrasyullus.

After the Athenians were so thoroughly defeated in 413, many Hellenes decided that it was time to revolt against Athens. When the citizens of the islands Lesbos and Euboea rebelled, they were encouraged by Agis II, who almost immediately summoned the general Alcamenes from Sparta to command the revolt. Nevertheless, the Erythraeans and the Chians sent envoys directly to Sparta seeking further military assistance, and these envoys were accompanied by a Persian satrap by the name of Tissaphernes, who had gained control over the Ionian coastal region after the satrap Pissuthenes had made an unsuccessful attempt at revolting against Darius II Nothus. Tissaphernes wanted the Spartan fleet to be the Persians' ally against the Athenians, which at that point retained control over a few strategic Hellenic cities in his territory.

Pharnabazus, who was the satrap of Hellespontine Phyrgia, also sent envoys to Sparta urging the Spartans to send their fleet directly to the Hellespont in order that they might begin to incite a rebellion there. However, in spite of their shared objective, the two satraps were actually at cross-purposes; each wanted to have exclusive control over the Greek cities in Asia Minor, but both knew that this goal could not be achieved without revolt.

The Persians found an unlikely ally in Alcibiades, who persuaded his friend Endius and a number of other Spartan ephors to make a vigorous resumption of their war against the Athenians across the Aegean Sea. Alcibiades furthermore swore that he would ignite a rebellion in Ionia and cement Persia's alliance with Sparta. Alcibiades made good on his word by sailing to Chios with five Spartan ships commanded by the Spartan general Chalcideus. There, he was able to persuade the Chians to revolt and secede from Athens.

Once ignited in Chios, the Ionian rebellion spread like wildfire. Next to secede were Anaea, Eresus, Methymna, Mytilene, Teos, Clazomenae, Erythrae, and Ephesus. As with the other cities, the revolt in Ephesus was preceded by a surge of clandestine correspondence with the other rebels, prompting the Greek tactician Aeneas Tacticus to note, "A man could be easily sent to Ephesus with a message written on leaves which were bound to a wound on his leg." Through the end of the Peloponnesian War, Ephesus would remain an effective ally for the Spartans.

It should come as no surprise that Alcibiades' rule in Ephesus and the nearby islands of Lesbos and Chios came to be characterized by corruption and wanton lawlessness. Andocides, an Athenian orator, recalls how the people of Ephesus erected for Alcibiades "a Persian pavilion twice as large as that of our official deputation." Andocides complained that Alcibiades was so lucky "that although the Greek people at large can testify to his lawlessness and corruption, he has gone unpunished. While those who hold office within a single city have to render account of that office, Alcibiades, whose authority extends over all our allies and who receives monies from them, is not liable to answer for any of his public acts…"

The Athenian response to the revolts in coastal Asia Minor was swift and immediate. The Athenian admirals Strombichides and Thrasycles promptly sailed their flotillas into the Aegean, where they intended to suppress the revolts and confront Chalcideus' fleet in battle. What Strombichides and Thrasycles did not know, however, was that Alcibiades and Chalcideus were no longer in Chios - they had already departed for Miletus, where they were able to successfully incite yet another revolt. Given its strategic central location in the southern Aegean islands and its excellent port facilities, Miletus quickly came to be an important Spartan naval base. The Spartans also benefited from Chalcideus' negotiations with Tissaphernes, which stipulated that Darius II would provide the Spartans with financial and military support against Athens in exchange for control over all the Hellenes who inhabited the Ionian cities.

Sparta's good fortune did not last for long. Agis II soon came to suspect that his son Leotychides was not actually legitimate but the entirely illegitimate seed of Agis' wife, Timaea, and Alcibiades. Accordingly, he ordered Alcibiades to be put to death. Alcibiades—of course—was not about to surrender himself to such a fate; instead, he betrayed Sparta in much the same way that he had betrayed Athens. Alcibiades told Tissaphernes that it would be ill-advised to prematurely end the Peloponnesian War by bringing in the Phoenician fleet that the Persians had been holding in reserve, and Alcibiades persuaded Tissaphernes that it would be advantageous to let the Spartans and the Athenians wear each other out first. Moreover, he encouraged Tissaphernes to be friendlier to the Athenians, as he was secretly hoping that he would be able to return to the Athenian side with immunity.

Alcibiades therefore sent word to the Athenians who were stationed on Samos, offering to make himself a friend to them and secure the Persians as their ally against the Spartans. Naturally, the Athenians did not trust Alcibiades, but they recognized that he might be able to bring them the Persian king's Phoenician ships. Thus, the Athenian general Thrasyllus decided to give Alcibiades what he wanted—full immunity—and appointed him admiral of the Athenian fleet at Samos. Alcibiades did not let him down; in his repeated engagements of the Spartan fleet, he was able to secure three great victories, first at Cynossema in 411, then at Abydos in the same year, and finally at Cyzicus in 410.

By 409, Thrasyllus had decided that he wanted to take Ephesus, and once he learned of Thrasyllus' intentions, Tissaphernes sent his horsemen to rally as many as he could to come to the defense of the city. Thrasyllus arrived in Ephesus with a sizable force, but defenders of Ephesus were ready for them. According to the Greek historian Xenophon, Thrasyllus, "having disembarked his hoplites at the foot of Mt. Koressus, and the cavalry, peltasts, marines, and all the rest near the marsh on the opposite side of the city, he led forward his two divisions at daybreak. The defenders of the city sallied forth to meet the attack—the Ephesians, the allies whom Tissaphernes had brought to them, the crews of the original twenty Syracusan ships under the command of Eucles, the son of Hippon, and Heracleides, the son of Aristogenes, and finally, the crews of two Selinuntine ships. All these contingents directed their first attacks upon the hoplites at Koressus; and after routing them, killing about a hundred of them, they turned their attention to those by the marsh: and there also the Athenians were put to flight, and about three hundred of them were killed. So the Ephesians set up a trophy there and a second [trophy] at Koressus."[3]

Alcibiades, however, was soon able to get his revenge. When 25 of the enemy ships attempted to sail from Ephesus, he swiftly captured four of them and managed to chase the rest back to Ephesus. Once Alcibiades had dealt with the Ephesians, he subdued Chalcedon and Byzantium before returning briefly to Athens in 408. There, he received a hero's welcome and was promoted to General-in-Chief, a title which came with absolute authority.

After his promotion, Alcibiades was eager to return to the waters of the Aegean, where he set about driving the Spartans from Miletus, Rhodes, Chios, Andros, Abydos, and Ephesus. In 407, the Spartans chose Lysander as the new commander of the Aegean fleet. Having arrived at Rhodes, Lysander sailed to Cos and Miletus. From Miletus, he then sailed to Ephesus, where he elected to move the Spartan command because he believed that Ephesus was better located than Miletus. In Lysander's judgment, "the position of the Milesian base south of Samos meant that any Spartan fleet headed for the Straits could be intercepted by the Athenians. Ephesus enjoyed one advantage—it was much closer to the provincial Persian capital of Sardis."

Once he had transferred the Spartan fleet to Ephesus, Lysander brought his ships ashore, as they were in crucial need of drying and repairs. His ships benched, Lysander began to take an interest in the commerce of Ephesus. According to the Greek biographer Plutarch, Lysander "found the city well inclined to the Spartans, but in a bad condition as to its internal policy, and in danger of falling into the barbarous manners of the Persians: because it was near Lydia, and the king's lieutenants often visited it. Lysander, therefore, having fixed his quarters there, ordered all his store-ships to be brought into their harbor and built a dock for his galleys. By these means, he filled their port with merchants, their markets with business, and their houses and shops with money: so that from time and from his services, Ephesus began to conceive hopes of greatness and splendor."[4]

---

[3] Xen. Hell. I.II.6-10
[4] Xen. Hell. I.II.11-12

At the same time, Lysander was enticed by all of the opulence surrounding him, and he soon fell into the barbarous manners of the Persians. Having rejected the ancient Spartan code of conduct as "burdensome," Lysander replaced his old ways with excessively luxurious habits. Before long, Lysander had even made an ally of Cyrus the Younger, the teenaged second son of King Darius II. The relationship between Lysander and Cyrus the Younger was a close one; according to the Greek geographer Pausinias, whenever Lysander asked Cyrus for money so that he could pay the Spartan fleet, Cyrus would promptly give it to him in full.

With such a promise of renewed Persian funding, Lysander felt confident enough to go on the offensive against the Athenians. In 406, Alcibiades, having learned that Lysander was in Ephesus fitting out his fleet, moved all his ships to Ephesus, but he failed to draw Lysander out for battle. By this point, Alcibiades was running low on supplies, so he decided to plunder the enemy's nearby coastal towns for provisions. Alcibiades left the command of his squadron to his boyhood friend Antiochus with strict orders not to participate in battle while he was away, but in an effort to insult Lysander, Antiochus decided to sail close to the harbor entrance of Ephesus. There, he attempted to display his prowess and bravery by hailing the Spartan fleet with a barrage of noise and laughter. A battle—provoked by rude gestures and insults—soon ensued, and according to Plutarch, "Lysander, resenting the affront, got a few of his ships under sail and gave chase; however, when he saw the Athenians coming to support Antiochus, he called up more of his galleys, and at last the action became general. Lysander gained the victory, took fifteen ships, and erected a trophy."

The disgrace gave the Athenians an excuse to remove Alcibiades from command. Dismissed from his position, Alcibiades was forced to seek refuge in the Chersonese. From here, he secured the protection of Pharnabazus, the Phrygian satrap, but in 404 he was murdered by some of Pharnabazus' men, perhaps on Lysander's orders. After the death of Alcibiades, Plutarch wrote that Lysander invited to Ephesus "the boldest and most enterprising inhabitants of the Greek cities in Asia and sowed among them the seeds of those aristocratic forms of government which afterwards took place. He encouraged them to enter into associations, and to turn their thoughts to politics, upon promise that when Athens was once subdued, the popular government in their cities too should be dissolved and the administration vested in them."[5]

At this point, however, Lysander's two-year term as admiral of the Spartan fleet had expired, so he was replaced by an upright Spartan named Callicratidas. Callicratidas almost immediately found himself in trouble with both Lysander and Cyrus the Younger. Like Lysander before him, Callicratidas wished to obtain pay for his men, so he sailed for Ephesus, where he demanded an instant audience with Cyrus the Younger. Callicratidas came to Cyrus unbidden, and so he sat unserved. Angered by what he perceived as an affront, Callicratidas sailed for Miletus, and there, he accused Miletus of returning unneeded surpluses to Cyrus the Younger. Eventually, Miletus provided Callicratidas with alternative funding, but even this could not save the unfortunate

---

[5] Plut. Lys.1.477a

Callicratidas. Later that year, Callicratidas decided to engage the Athenian fleet off the coast of the Arginusae islets in what would become the largest naval battle of the Peloponnesian War. After a fierce battle, the Spartans were thoroughly defeated by the Athenian fleet. To make matters worse, the seas were especially stormy, and after the battle, Callicratidas fell overboard and drowned.

After Callicradtidas' untimely death, Lysander was re-appointed commander of the Spartan fleet, and almost immediately, he engaged the Athenian fleet of almost 200 ships on the beaches of Aegospotami in battle. Lysander was victorious, and the Ephesians in commemoration erected a statue of Lysander in the Temple of Artemis. Alongside this statue of Lysander stood statues of Pharax, Eteonicus, and a number of other Spartans whose importance was not imparted to the greater Greek world.

With Lysander's victory at Aegospotami, the last fleet that the Athenians could equip in the Peloponnesian fleet had been destroyed; by this point, the Athenians could no longer even sustain their city with a supply of corn from the east. Philocles, the commander-in-chief of the Athenian fleet, was brutally slaughtered and denied a proper burial, an egregious offense to the Athenians, who had taken care to give a proper burial to even the Persians at Marathon. To add insult to injury, Lysander ordered that those whom he had taken capture "have their right hands cut off as an awful punishment and warning."

Next, Lysander moved on to Athens, where he laid siege to the city and starved its citizens. In 404, Lysander subjected Athens to the ruthless oligarchic dictatorship of the "thirty tyrants." These tyrants—led by an orator named Critias (the uncle of Plato)—carried out an unyielding policy of confiscation, murder, and general terror. In 403, however, the Athenians killed Critias and managed to restore their democracy. Not long afterwards, in 395, Lysander was slain by Thebans when he attempted to lay siege to the Boeotian city of Haliartus. According to the Samian chronicler Duris, "Lysander was the first Greek to whom cities set up altars to as a god and made sacrifice,"[6] though the tyrant of Ephesus Athenagoras added that they did so "notwithstanding all the slaughters and all the crimes perpetuated by him."[7]

In the meantime, Artaxerxes II, planning an expedition against his brother Arsaces, approached the Spartans, urging them "to send him men, promising to give horses to their foot-soldiers, chariots to those who had horses, villages to those who owned farms, and to those who had villages, the masters of cities, and as for gold and silver there should be no counting, but weighing instead." The Spartans, thinking that the war would be to their advantage, decided to send 25 triremes and 800 infantry soldiers to Ephesus. The Spartan forces were ready to cooperate with Cyrus the Younger in absolutely every respect. For his part, Cyrus set forth with an army of mercenary soldiers. When Cyrus the Younger arrived at the Gates between Syria and

---
[6] Plut. Lys.18.5
[7] Athenagoras Leg. pro Christ 14

Cicilia, he sent word to Ephesus that part of the fleet was still with him.

For his part, Tissaphernes had gone to Artaxerxes II, informing him of Cyrus the Younger's intent. Before the year of 401 was through, Artaxerxes II had defeated Cyrus' expedition at the Battle of Cunaxa on the Euphrates River at Bagdad, and Cyrus the Younger was killed by a javelin-blow. After the Battle of Cunaxa, Tissaphernes entered into false negotiations with a Macedonian commander named Clearchus. Having trapped the Macedonian generals, Tissaphernes put them to death on the order of Artaxerxes II.

By 396, the Spartan King Agesilaus II, who had been the successor of Agis II, had gathered the entirety of his army at Ephesus, where he intended to fight Tissaphernes. Agesilaus II was able to secure an easy victory over Tissaphernes. Artaxerxes II, frightened by just how easily Tissaphernes was defeated, ordered the satrap to be assassinated, and he replaced Tissaphernes with a Persian named Tiribazus, who immediately came up with a plan to force the Spartans to recall their army from Asia. Tiribazus financed a Rhodian named Timocrates and sent him to Greece, where he was instructed to incite a war against the Spartans.

The Corinthian War (395-386) was the direct result of Persia's clandestine activities in Greece. The incipient war forced Agesilaus II to abandon his victories in Asia and engage the Persian allies in mainland Greece. In 394, Pharnabazus' fleet—then commanded by the Athenian Conon—was able to annihilate the Spartan fleet off the coast of the island Cnidus. As a consequence of this victory, the Persians were able to expel the Spartan rulers from Asia Minor's coastal cities.

The Ephesians, tired of Spartan hegemony, began deserting to Conon's anti-Spartan maritime league. The other cities in Ionia quickly followed suit, and the Spartan garrison was soon expelled from the region. In 392, the Spartans dispatched a general named Thibron to reestablish control in Asia Minor, but the Athenian satrap Struthas quickly put an end to their ambitions by defeating the Spartan force in the Maeander Valley, just a short distance from Ephesus.

After this Athenian victory, the Spartans and the Athenians negotiated a peace, thereby bringing the Corinthian War to an end. Having arrived at Aegina in 389, the Spartan diplomat Antalicidas was immediately transported to Ephesus by Gorgopas, who was the vice-admiral of the Spartan fleet. There, Antalicidas entered into negotiations with the Persians. Plutarch, calling the affair a "disreputable business," describes how in 388, Antalicidas "surrendered into the Persian king's power those Greeks in Asia Minor for whose freedom Agesilaus II had fought." Thus, Ephesus and its neighbors suddenly found themselves once again under the Persian yoke.

In 371, a "sacred band" under the command of the Theban general Epaminodas thoroughly defeated Agesilaus II at the Battle of Leuctra. A decade of successful Theban expeditions into the Peloponnese ensued, effectively ending Spartan control of the region, but in the meantime, Artaxerxes II had come to be concerned with an uprising of several satraps. Twice these belligerent satraps attacked Ephesus. According to the Greek historian Polyaenus, the first of these two attacks occurred when the satrap Mausolus (377–353) set out on a march to Latmus on his way to Pygela, a coastal city which was located between Neapolis and Ephesus. On his way, he attempted to take control of Ephesus from its tyrant, Herophytus, who had recently renounced his allegiance to Mausolus. As soon as Mausolus tried to enter Ephesus, Herophytus drove him back. Herophytus died in the skirmish, but he succeeded in saving his city, and in order to show their gratitude, the Ephesians buried him in the Ephesian agora.

In 365, the renegade satrap Autophradates—also on his way through Ionia—decided to attack Ephesus. Autophradates "observed that the Ephesians, who were encamped opposite him, were walking around in a leisurely fashion and relaxing. While he was thus engaged with them, the generals of his cavalry and hoplites, according to the orders which he had given them, suddenly attacked the Ephesians, who were dispersed in straggling groups and unprepared for action. Some of them were cut down and the rest were made prisoners."[8]

In approximately 360, the Satrap of Cilicia, Datames, was assassinated, and the Satrap's Revolt was brought to an end.

Chapter 4: Alexander the Great

---

[8] Polyaenus. Straegemata 7.27.2

Philip II of Macedon

Alexander the Great

While the satraps were being finished off, Philip II, who had just been released from captivity in Thebes, was appointed regent of Macedonia. Three years later, his wife, Olympias, gave birth to a baby boy, whom they named Alexander, and on the very same day, a man named Herostratus intentionally burned down the Temple of Artemis in Ephesus. According to Plutarch, "All the Magi, who were then at Ephesus, looked upon the fire as a sign which betokened a much greater misfortune: they ran about the town, beating their faces and crying 'that they day had brought forth the great scourge and destroyer of Asia.'"

Though some of the Ephesians would later blame the goddess for being away to attend the birth of Alexander, Herostratus was immediately condemned. Some citizens who claimed to have witnessed the unfortunate event even claimed that Herostratus "went up and down proclaiming that he was the man who had applied the fire." It was speculated that Herostratus, unable to attain fame in any other way, had set the ancient temple aflame in order to make a name for himself. Though the Ephesians issued a decree abolishing the memory of the villain, history has not yet been able to forget Herostratus and his perverse legacy.

While the Ephesians mourned the attack on their temple, Philip II, having secured the safety of his kingdom and reorganized his armies, took total control of the cities Potidae, Philippi, and Amphipolis. Not content with these gains, he eliminated the Chalcidian League and mounted an attack on Thrace. Unable to ignore the threat of Philip's increasing military might, Thebes and Athens declared war on the Macedonian regent, but in 338 the Greeks were thoroughly defeated at the Battle of Chaeronea in Boeotia. After the Battle of Chaeronea, Philip, having declared himself master of all of Greece, formed a Corinthian League of Greek city-states under Macedonian hegemony, united against the Persian enemy.

With the successful strategies of Agesilaus II in mind, Philip II launched an invasion of Asia Minor, which was then under the control of the Persian King Artaxerxes III (359–338). The Greek cities of Asia Minor sent an Ephesian emissary to Artaxerxes III expressing the region's support for the war Philip II was openly planning. This emissary—named Dias—was an avid follower of Plato and an ardent supporter of Philip's war against the barbarians. According to Philostratus, "When Dias saw that Philip was treating the Greeks harshly, he persuaded him to lead an expedition against Asia Minor, and went to and fro telling the Greeks that they ought to accompany Philip on his expedition, since it was no dishonor to endure slavery abroad in order to secure freedom at home." In order to prepare for this expedition of Asia Minor, Philip II sent forth about 10,000 of his men under the command of a Macedonian general named Parmenio. Having crossed the Hellespont, the troops moved south and entered Ephesus without resistance. There, they erected in the Temple of Artemis a statue of Philip II.

As fate would have it, Philip II never saw this statue because he was slain by an assassin in 336 before he could cross the Hellespont, but Philip's young son, Alexander, was eager to pursue his father's plans. In 336, Alexander crossed the Dardanelles from Eleus to Troy with 5,000 cavalry, 30,000 infantry, and approximately 160 ships. It was his mission to wage a war of vengeance against the Persians in order to win retribution for the wrongs that Xerxes I had committed against the Greeks nearly 150 years prior. Once he arrived in Asia Minor, he "flung his spear from the ship and fixed it to the ground, and then leapt ashore…signifying that he had received Asia from the gods as a spear-won prize."[9]

Almost immediately, Alexander took control of the cities that were located along the northern seaboard of Asia Minor, including Dascylium, Cyzicus, and Lampsacus. Indeed, Alexander did

---

[9] Diod. Sic. XVII.18.2-21.7

not pass through a single city without liberating it from the Persians, overthrowing its oligarchy, and establishing a new democracy. Proceeding southward, Alexander crushed the troops the Persian King Darius had position at the river Granicus. Next, Alexander moved through Mysia towards Ephesus, pursuing a band of retreating Persian mercenaries under the command of the Persian general Memnon. When the news of the Persian defeat at Granicus reached the mercenary troops stationed at Ephesus, the mercenaries immediately fled for Halicarnassus in two Ephesian triremes.

Upon arriving in Ephesus, Alexander recalled every man who had been banished from the city because they had supported him. Once he had broken up the pro-Persian oligarchy, Alexander—as per his custom—re-established the government in the form of a democracy. Additionally, he ordered the Ephesians to re-allocate the money they had been paying the barbarians to a temple-tax for the goddess Artemis. No longer restrained by their fears of the pro-Persian oligarchy, the Ephesians hastened to kill those who had invited Memnon into their city. Not yet content, they also sought the blood of those who had pillaged the Temple of Artemis after Herostratus burned it down, those who had defaced the temple's statue of Philip II, and those who had dug up the tomb of Herophytus, who had once liberated Ephesus.

In this mad bloodlust, the Ephesians even dared to disregard the inviolability of the Temple of Artemis. The pro-Persian tyrant Syrphax and his young son Pelagon had sought refuge inside the temple, but this did not stop the vengeful Ephesians from pulling them out of the temple and stoning them to death. After witnessing this brutal scene, Alexander put an end to any further inquiry or punishment, as he knew that the people of Ephesus in their current mentality would put innocent men to death along with the guilty. The historian Arrian wrote that "seldom did Alexander win a higher reputation than he did on that occasion by his fair treatment of Ephesus." Alexander even offered to rebuild the Temple of Artemis, but the Ephesians refused to let him on the alleged grounds that a god could not build a temple for a god. Still, before departing Ephesus, Alexander made a ritual sacrifice to Artemis and held a great procession with his armed troops in full battle order. After his departure, the city of Ephesus entered a much-needed period of relative peace.

When they left Ephesus, Alexander marched south to Miletus. Having taken the city, he disbanded all but 20 Athenian ships of his fleet and pursued Memnon by land to the Dorian city of Halicarnassus. By 334, Alexander had forced the Persians to evacuate Halicarnassus, and after Alexander conquered what was left of Halicarnassus, Darius III appointed Memnon "controller of lower Asia" and "commander of the fleet." Darius III instructed Memnon to divert Alexander from his true purpose by carrying the war over into Greece and Macedonia, effectively making a fourth Persian attempt on Greece.

As had become evident in the wars of the past centuries, the first step in any successful campaign against the Greek mainland was to reduce the islands of the eastern Aegean Sea. By this point, Samos and Cos had already come over to Darius III, and Chios was quick to follow its neighbors.

It is not unlikely that Memnon requested the help of the Spartan King Agis III, because not long after Darius III began taking the islands of the Aegean, Agis III began to lead a revolt of the Peloponnesian cities with the intent of liberating Greece from Macedonian hegemony. Before the Persian forces could pose any serious threat to Alexander, however, Memnon died, and Darius III's Hellenic military ambitions died with him.

After conquering Halicarnassus, Alexander proceeded inland through Pamphylia and Cilicia to the Issus River. There, he managed to confront and defeat the Persian army, but he did not succeed in capturing Darius III. From the Issus River, Alexander moved south along the coast of Palestine to Egypt. Along his way, he captured Gaza, Tyre, Aradus, Byblos, and Sidon. In 332 , he founded the city of Alexandria in Egypt on the ancient site of Paros, and from Alexandria, Alexander backtracked to Tyre, whence he began his campaign in the east. Having set forth from Tyre and Damascus, Alexander advanced his troops to Thapsacus, where he crossed the Euphrates and the Tigris. Alexander soon defeated Darius' army once again at Gaugamela, and Darius, almost eluding him once again, was promptly captured and killed in Media.

In 327 , Alexander was moving eastward through Parthia to Sangalae. At the young age of 32, when he should have been just reaching the zenith of his power and glory, Alexander died in Babylon, after he had conquered Gedrosia, Gandhara, Sogdiana, Bacrtia, Drangiana, Arachosia, Aria, Parthia, Persia, Media, Babylon, Assyria, Egypt, Phoenicia, Syria, and Asia Minor. The exact cause of his death remains unknown.

Also unknown is the reason that Alexander the Great never chose a successor to rule over his unprecedentedly vast empire in the event of his death. Alexander the Great had a mentally slow half-brother—Philip II Arrhideus—who was unfit to rule and an unborn child—Alexander IV—who was in time expected to become his heir and successor. In the meantime, however, Alexander the Great had clearly not trusted any of his generals enough to allow them to become even temporary regent. Perdiccas, Alexander's vizier, assumed control of the emperor as regent, but his rule was almost immediately challenged by a more experienced general named Antipater. Soon, a number of generals found themselves vying for control over Alexander's extensive conquests.

322 thus saw the beginning of The War of the Successors. During the first period of the war (321–301), Antigonus I led the unitarians (those who wanted to preserve the unity of the empire) against the separatists (those who wanted to carve out their own kingdoms). In order to ensure that he had a strong base in Ionia, Antigonus I, aided by confederates within the city, took Ephesus, and by 315 Antigonus I had achieved a position of primacy in Asia Minor. Not yet content with his lot, Antigonus sent his general Demetrius forth in order to liberate all of the cities in Greece from the rule of his separatist enemies, and for the next several years, control of

mainland Greece and the coastal cities of Asia Minor volleyed back and forth between the unitarian general Demetrius and the separatist general Lysimachus.

During his occupancy of the city, Lysimachus devoted himself to completely transforming Ephesus. Most notably, he reformed the Ephesian senate to a conscripted Senate associated with the Epicleti, who administered the city's affairs. The new senate passed a number of measures to mitigate the debt Ephesus had accumulated in its recent wars. Even more significantly, Lysimachus decided to move the location of the city away from its old site near the Temple of Artemis to a new site that was located approximately 2.5 kilometers southwest of the Temple in the valley that lay between Mount Pion and Mount Koresis. Ephesus' port had come to be blocked by a massive amount of alluvial silt, and the land had begun to convert into marsh, making the city's old location no longer viable.

Of course, the citizens of Ephesus were unwilling to leave behind their old city. Lysimachus thus waited for a torrential downpour, and when the rains came, he blocked the waterways and sewers, inundating the city and rendering its houses uninhabitable. The Ephesians thus had no choice but to move to the site of their new city, which Lysimachus dubbed Arsinoeia.

Lysimachus then set about constructing a new harbor for his new city and enclosed the city with a new defensive wall that ran down to the harbor. Some ancient historians claim that the wall's two-storied guard tower was erected upon the ancient foundation of the so-called "Tower of Treason" that had once been attacked by Croesus when Ephesus was under the rule of the tyrant Pindar.

Lysimachus is often credited with the construction of Ephesus' Great Theater, but there is almost no evidence supporting the claim that he was responsible for its initial phase of construction. Nevertheless, several historians suspect that it may have been Lysimachus who was responsible for choosing the theater's location - the side of a steep hill in what was then the center of the "new" ancient city - at some point prior to his death in 281 Initially, the Great Theater featured one cavea[10] with one row of seats, a modest one-story stage house, and an orchestra with a drainage channel. The theater would be greatly expanded during Rome's reign.

It is estimated that the Magnesia Gate, which served as the southeastern entrance to Ephesus, was constructed at approximately the same time. The Magnesia Gate, named for the nearby town of Magnesia-on-the-Meander, was erected in the Doric order and featured a square courtyard on the city side of the nearly 12 foot passageway.

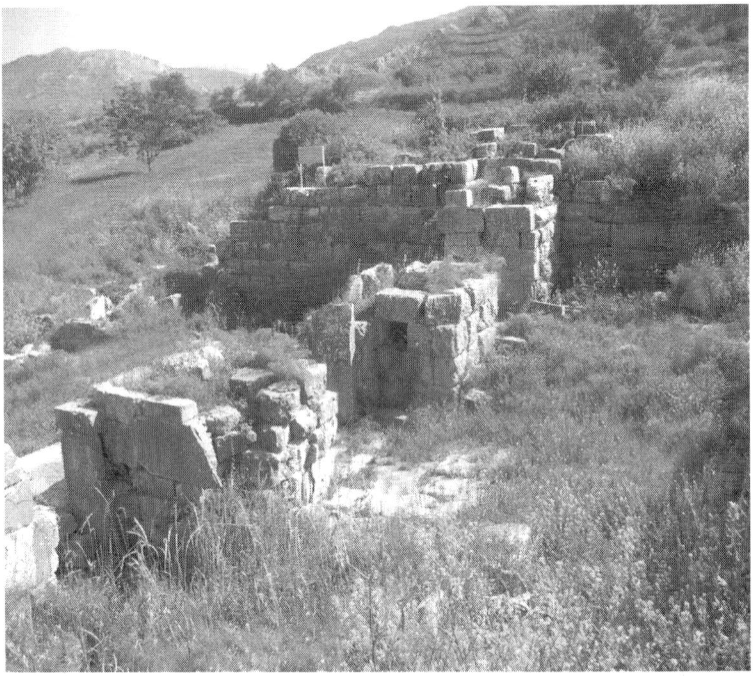

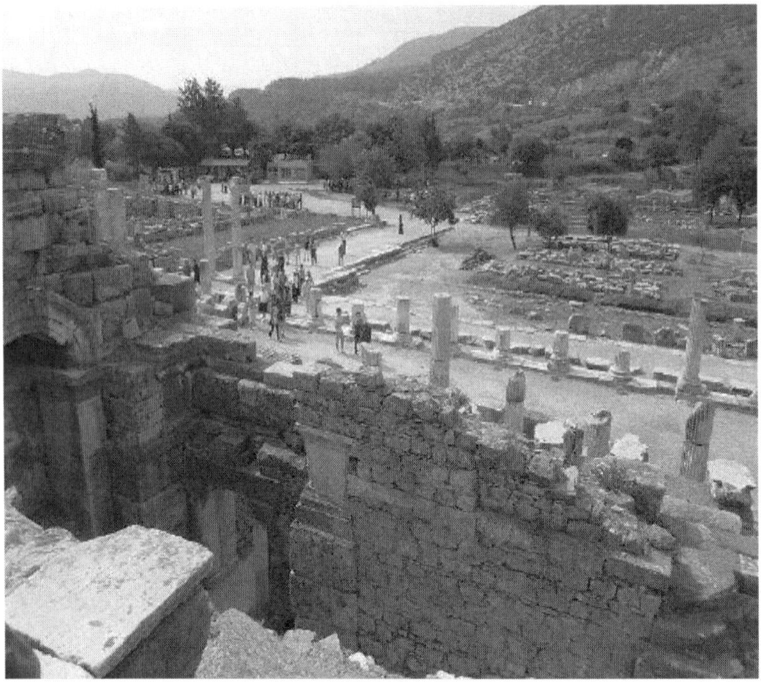

The ruins of the Magnesia Gate

In 281, Seleucus I, who had previously served Alexander the Great as a general, killed Lysimachus in single combat at the Battle of Corupedium near Magnesia. Consequently, Seleucus gained control of all Asia Minor, but before he could add any more territory to his empire, however, Seleucus was assassinated. Lysimachus' wife, Arsinoe, feared that Ephesus would be seized by Seleucus' followers, so she exchanged clothes with one of her slaves and managed to escape the city, and Seleucus's men killed the slave girl instead of Arsinoe. Arsinoe then went on to become queen by marrying her brother, Ptolemy II Philadelphus, the son of Ptolemy I Soter, another general of Alexander's.

Ephesus remained loyal to Ptolemy II until approximately 260, when Ptolemy Nios, the commander of an Ephesian guard, colluded with Timarchus, the tyrant of Miletus, in staging a revolt against Ptolemy II. The revolt was short-lived, as Ptolemy Nios was slain by his own Thracian mercenaries in 259 while he was fleeing to Ephesus, where he intended to seek refuge in the Temple of Artemis. Egyptian hegemony in Asia Minor was considerably weakened, and Seleucus's grandson, Antiochus II, was able to take control of coastal Ionia.

Though Ptolemy II and Antiochus II managed to negotiate a tentative peace in 253, tensions between their respective empires remained high, and by 246, war had broken out once again. Considerable trouble at home forced Ptolemy III, who had by then taken the Egyptian throne, to cease his advance. Seleucus II, having thus retained control over the Orontes River region, kept a sizable military force at Ephesus, but in 243, Ptolemy III managed to take Ephesus and regain control of southern Asia Minor. The Ptolemies and the Seleucids grappled for control of the region until 198, when Antiochus III routed Ptolemy V's forces at the Battle of Panuim and thereby secured control over the cities of Asia Minor.

Chapter 4: Roman Ephesus

Around the time Antiochus III established Seleucid dominance in the region, the exiled Carthaginian general Hannibal arrived in Ephesus, where he succeeded in inciting Antiochus III against the increasingly powerful city of Rome. For their part, the Roman Senate sent a commission to Ephesus in order to get a feel for the situation there, and perhaps not surprisingly, the Roman commission left Ephesus deeply concerned about Hannibal's possible involvement with Antiochus given what the Carthaginian had done during the Second Punic War.

Hannibal. (Neapel, National-Museum.)

Hannibal

Before long, Antiochus III saw fit to go to war with Rome on the pretense that he was liberating Greece from its conquerors, so in 191, the Roman Senate reciprocated by declaring war on Antiochus III, who by that point had become smitten with a young daughter of the Chalcidian Cleoptolemus. Overcome by desire, Antiochus III no longer had any interest in his war effort. Instead, "he proceeded to celebrate a wedding, as though peace were established all around. Forgetting the importance of the two causes he had taken up together, the war with Rome and the liberation of Greece, the king abandoned responsibility for everything and spent the rest of the winter in dinner-parties, and the pleasures that go along with drinking."[11]

After staging an effective blockade of Ephesus' harbor, the Roman armada defeated

---
[11] Livy XXXVI.11

Antiochus' fleet at the Battle of Myonnesus near Ephesus in 190, and shortly thereafter, Antiochus' army was defeated at the Battle of Magnesia ad Sipylum. In 188, the Romans dispatched a second commission to Ephesus, and the commission proceeded from Ephesus to Syria, where they negotiated a comprehensive peace treaty (the Treaty of Apamea) giving the Romans political hegemony in the eastern Mediterranean.

Following the Treaty of Apamea, Ephesus came to be controlled by Eumenes II, a member of the Attalid dynasty that had ruled Pergamon ever since the death of Lysimachus in 281. Recognizing Ephesus' commercial importance, Eumenes' successor, Attalus II, ordered Ephesus' harbor basin drained and commissioned the construction of new breakwaters. According to the ancient geographer Strabo, "the mouth of the harbor was made narrower by the engineers, but they, along with the king who ordered it, were deceived as to the result…Attalus thought that the entrance would be deep enough for large merchant vessels—as also the harbor itself, which formerly had shallow places because of the silt deposited by the Cayster River—if a mole were thrown up at the mouth, which was very wide, and therefore ordered that the mole should be built. But the result was the opposite, for the silt, thus hemmed in, made the whole harbor, as far as the mouth, shallower."[12] Attalus' attempt at dredging Ephesus' harbor was nothing more than an inefficient measure designed to postpone the problem of its ongoing silting and thus prolong the lifespan of what was now the largest commercial emporium in Asia Minor on the western side of the Taurus River.

Attalus II died in 138 and rule passed to his son, Attalus III, who had no children of his own. He thus returned the Kingdom of Pergamum to the Romans, who readily incorporated the Attalid territory into their ever-expanding empire. The consul Manius Aquillius named the addition "Provincia Asia" and built within it the region's first Roman roads. Ephesus, which for administrative purposes now included 23 cities in its judicial circuit, had a population of approximately 215,000 citizens and became the capital of this new province and the seat of its Roman governor.

The Roman mercilessly exploited their territories in Asia Minor for their own financial gain until the beginning of the 1st century BCE, when Mithridates VI, the king of Pontus and Armenia Minor, sensed the frustration of the Ephesians as an opportunity to expand his own kingdom. He incited a war with Rome's allies and quickly moved into Asia Minor, and when he arrived in Ephesus, the Ephesians welcomed him by overthrowing every Roman statue in the city.

---

[12] Strab. XIV.I.24

Mithridates VI

In 88, Mithridates signed a decree that ordered every Roman resident and collaborator in Asia Minor to be put to the death. Appian, a Roman historian, noted, "Mithridates wrote secretly to all his satraps and city governors that on the 30th day thereafter they should set upon the Romans and Italians in their towns, and upon their wives and children, and their freedmen of Italian birth, kill them, throw their bodies out unburied, and share their goods with King Mithridates. The Ephesians tore away the fugitives, who had taken refuge in the Temple of Artemis, and were clasping the images of the goddess, and slew them. Such was the awful fate that befell the Romans and Italians in Asia…by which it was made very clear that it was as much hatred of the Romans that impelled the Asians to commit these atrocities."[13]

---

[13] Appian. Mithridatic Wars. 12.4.22-23

The Roman historian Valerius Maximus estimates that 80,000 Roman businessmen were slain in the massacre, and in a supremely ironic gesture, Mithridates, who had not spared the Romans seeking refuge at the Temple of Artemis, granted additional rights of asylum to the temple by extending the sanctuary's limit as a shelter of protection to the length an arrow could fly from its pediment.

In 87 , the Roman consul Sulla entered into negotiations with Mithridates at Dardanus, thus temporarily ending the First Mithridatic War. Mithridates consequently retreated from Asia Minor, departing Ephesus in 86, and Sulla managed to recover Ephesus for Rome in 84. Perhaps not surprisingly, those who had sided with Mithridates and revolted against Rome were immediately put to death, and Sulla proceeded to strip Ephesus of its freedom and impose the exaction of a fine. Several decades later, during the reign of Augustus, the Romans erected in Ephesus a monument that depicted Sulla's capture of the city.

Sulla

Rome spent much of the ensuing decade at war with Mithridates until the Pontian king's army was at last thoroughly defeated by the Roman general Lucius Licinius Lucullus in 72. Not long after the end of the Mithridatic Wars, Rome found itself embroiled in civil strife, first between Julius Caesar and Pompey the Great, then between Caesar's heir Octavian and Mark Antony. Even distant Ephesus felt the ramifications of the conflict; in an absolutely unprecedented move, Pompey plundered the common treasury of Asia, which was under the protection of the goddess Artemis and housed in her Ephesian Temple. A few decades later, Antony, seeking revenues for his own war, came to Ephesus with his Egyptian consort Cleopatra. Anthony is said to have entered Ephesus styling himself as "a harbinger of life an all good things." According to

Plutarch, "When Anthony entered Ephesus, the women in the dress of Bacchanals, and men and boys habited like Pan and satyrs, marched before him. Nothing was to be seen through the whole city but ivy crowns and spears wreathed with ivy, harps, flutes, and pipes, while Antony was hailed by the name of Bacchus: 'Bacchus! Ever kind and free!'"[14]

Antony

Of course, the support of Ephesus was not enough for Anthony. In 31, Octavian defeated Anthony and Cleopatra at the Battle of Actium, after which the two committed suicide. Rome

---

[14] Plutarch. Anthony. II.976b.

was now officially an empire, and Octavian, who would henceforth be known as Augustus, was at its helm.

Augustus

Near the end of his life, Augustus famously claimed that he found Rome "a city of brick and left it a city of marble," and he was committed to a massive program of building and restoration throughout his empire. In Ephesus, he "gave permission for the dedication of sacred precincts…to Roma and to Caesar his father, whom he named the hero Iulus." Additionally, he "replaced in the temples in all the cities of the province of Asia the ornaments which Antony, in the war, when he despoiled the temples, appropriated to his own use."[15] Augustus also bestowed citizenship upon the Jews of Ephesus, who by this point made up a significant portion of the city's population.

By the year 1 CE, Ephesus had entered an era of unprecedented prosperity and prominence; with the patronage of the great Roman Empire, Ephesus became a bustling commercial hub, known as the "First and Greatest Metropolis of Asia." Moreover, Roman patrons began adding to Ephesus' state agora (marketplace) in order to accommodate the new political, commercial, social, and religious needs of the city. A rectangular temple on the agora's western end that may have once been dedicated to the Egyptian goddess Isis when Ephesus belonged to the Ptolemies was re-dedicated to Augustus. To the north of the agora, the Romans erected their own temples to Divus Iulius and Dea Roma. An old building that had once been known as the Pritaneion was rebuilt to better serve Ephesus as its town hall and guest house. After renovation, the Pritaneion also functioned as a dining hall, an assembly hall, and an administrative center, and the Doric columns that supported the Pritaneion's lintels were engraved with depictions of the mysteries of Artemis. The Romans also destroyed a Hellenic hall on the northern border of the state agora in order to make room for a new basilica that featured three aisles, a nave, and Ionic columns decorated with bulls' heads.

Moving northwest from the state agora was a bustling street known at Curetes Street or the Embolos. Curetes Street joined the state agora to the "lower" agora, which was the commercial agora. The city's Roman elite favored Curetes Street as the location for their well-stuccoed marble villas. According to Biblical archaeologists John Crossan and Jonathan Reed, these homes "slope[d] upward on a terrace, and those on the lowest level have shops and taverns fronting the Curetes Street…pedestrians on that same street or along one of its steep alleys caught passing glimpses of wealth and decoration inside those villas. They saw marble and mosaic floors, walls painted with faux marble in geometric and floral patterns, and rich religious or cultural decorations. They say a niche with Dionysos's wedding to Ariadne in glass mosaic, Pan and Satyr associates of the wine god in a vaulted ceiling's stucco, and a painted bust of the philosopher Socrates. They saw, a set of panels depicting Apuleiu's religious-erotic novel The Golden Ass, a tale of one believer's conversion and initiation into the worship of the Egyptian mother goddess Isis."[16]

---

[15] Res Gestae Divi Augusti IV.23
[16] Crossan, J.D. and J.L. Reed. In Search of Paul (2004). 314-315.

Ronan Reinart's picture of excavated terrace houses from the Roman period

The entrance to the lower agora itself was marked by a three-gated monumental arch. The arch, most commonly known as the Gate of Mazaeus and Mithridates, was named after two of Augustus' freedmen, who, having moved to Euphesus upon their manumission, erected the gate in honor of their former master. The gate's inscription reads as follows: "[F]rom the Emperor Caesar Augustus, the son of the god, the greatest of the priests, who was consul twelve and tribune twenty times and the wife of August Livia: the son of Lucus, Marc Agrippa who was consul three times, emperor, and tribune six times: and the daughter of Julio Caesar Augustus, Mazaeus and Mithridates to their master and the people."

The Gate of Mazaeus and Mithridates Gate in Ephesus

The western side of the lower agora featured a gate that led out to Ephesus' West Street, which in turn led out to the Ephesian harbor.

As the Augustan era drew to a close, the Romans broke ground on a memorial that paid tribute to Sulla's military victories. The memorial, which faced the Embolos, was elevated on a pedestal and accessible via steps on each of its four sides. In traditional Roman style, it featured arches and semicircular naves that were decorated with block figures depicting the man of honor. Adjoined to the monument's northwestern side was a large fountain.

By the time the monument to Sulla was complete in the mid-1st century CE, the Embolos had come to be packed with all kinds of column-fronted shops, magnificent terrace villas, Roman bathhouses, an array of stately temples and tombs, and countless honorific statues and monuments dedicated to Roman officials and other elite citizens.

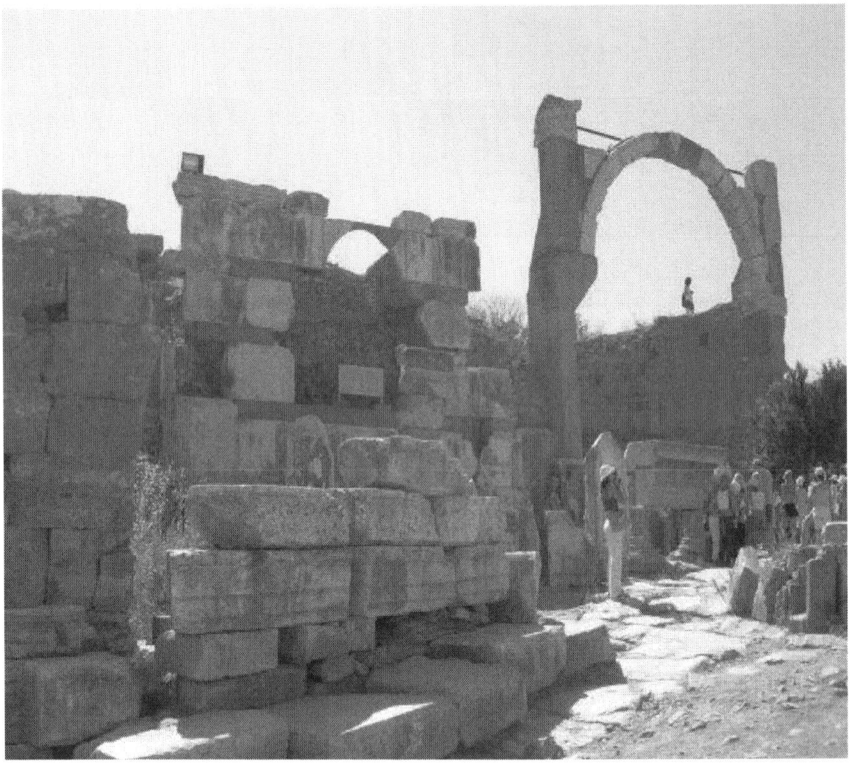

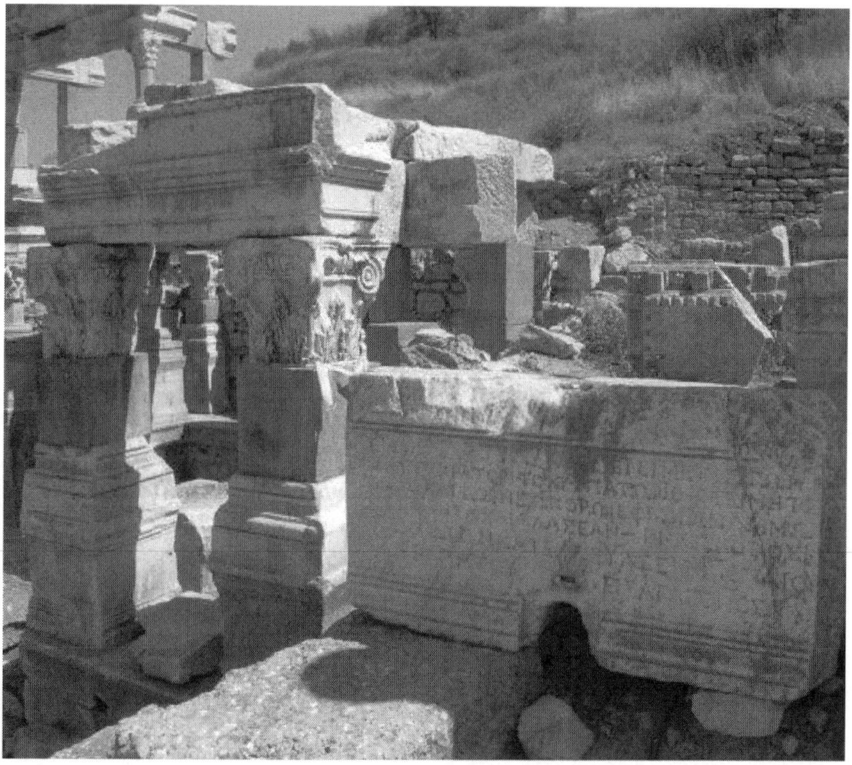

Pictures of the ruins of the Bath of Varius

Augustus died in 14 CE, believed by many to have been poisoned by his wife Livia, and after his death, Ephesus was shaken by a number of earthquakes, which prompted Augustus' successor Tiberius to commit to rebuilding in Asia Minor. However, new building projects in Ephesus were put on hold until the reign of Claudius (41–54), who was responsible for significantly enlarging the theater that was purportedly built by Lysimachus. Claudius rearranged the seats of the Great Theater so as to improve its acoustics and also enlarged its podium. Claudius' successor Nero then enlarged the stage house, bringing its total number of rooms to eight.

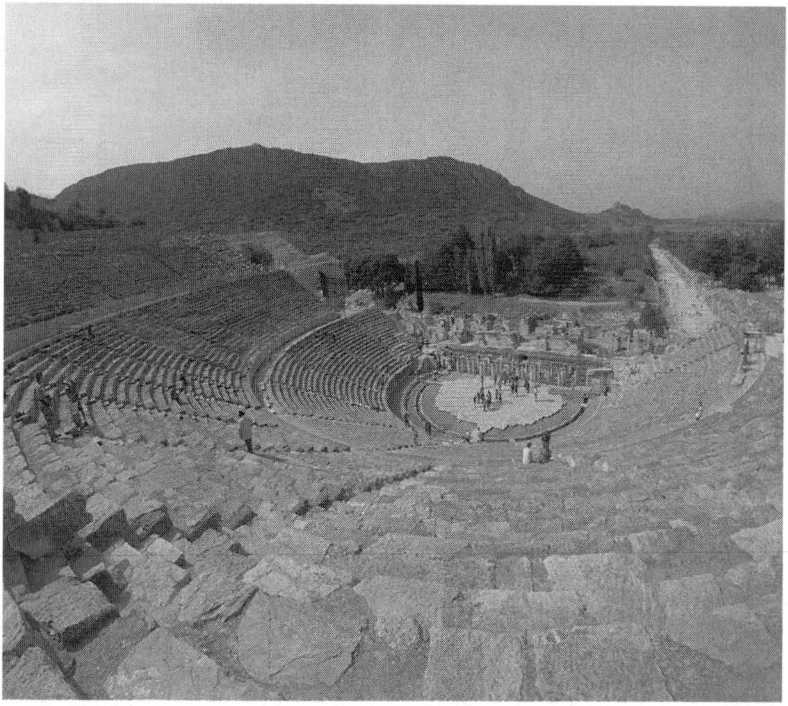

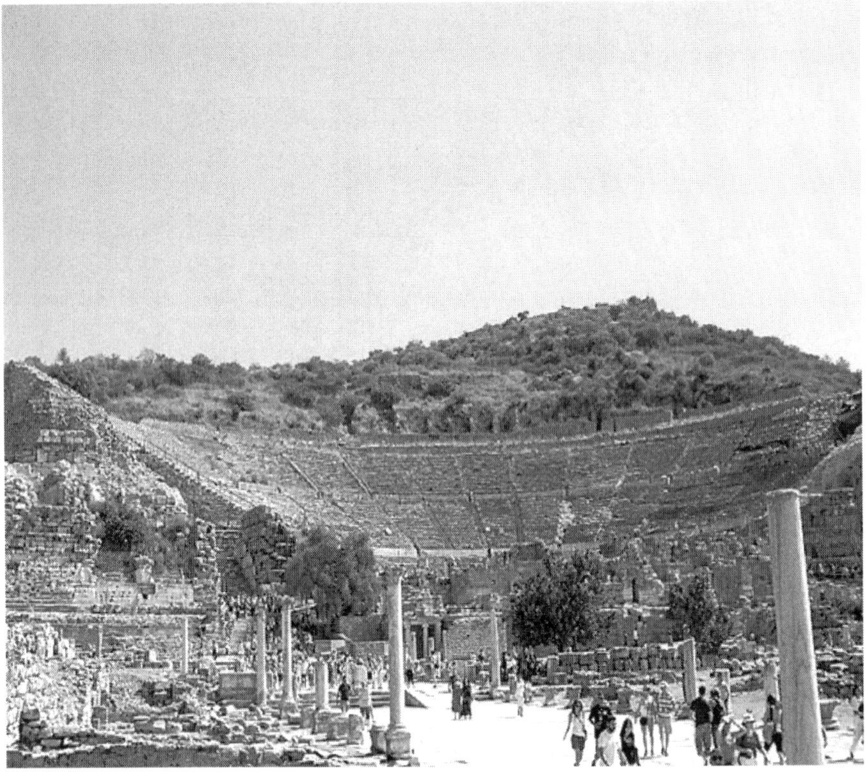

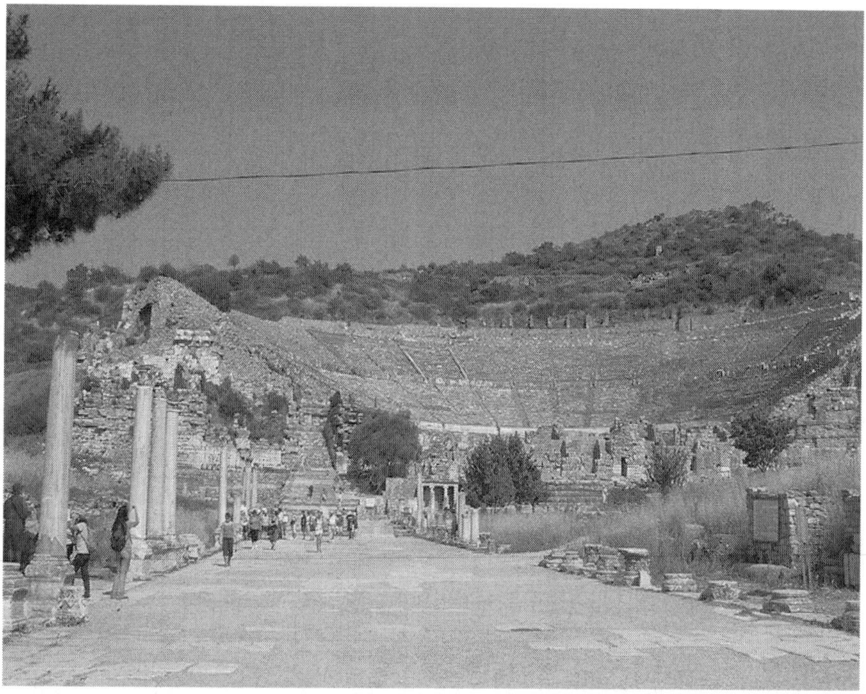

Pictures of the Ephesian theater

Nero was also responsible for the construction of Ephesus' Oval Stadium, a massive structure located just inside of the Koressus Gate that contained seats for approximately 75,000 spectators. The stadium's eastern end was designed so that its semicircular eastern end could be shut off and used as a stand-alone amphitheater for gladiatorial contests, and, occasionally, the ever-popular camel wrestling competition.

The Flavian emperors who succeeded Nero in 68 were not particularly interested in Ephesus until the emperor Domitian, who in approximately 89 C.E. declared that half of Asia Minor's vineyards should be uprooted in order to protect the interests of Italian winegrowers. The Ephesians especially balked at this new measure, and due to its unpopularity and difficulty of enforcement, Domitian revoked his edict. As a gesture of goodwill, he also appointed Ephesus as the protector of the emperor's temple (*neokoros*). The appointment prompted the erection of a neokoros Temple of Domitian, a pro-style ornamental temple that sat upon a three-storied walled terrace and contained the cult image of the emperor.

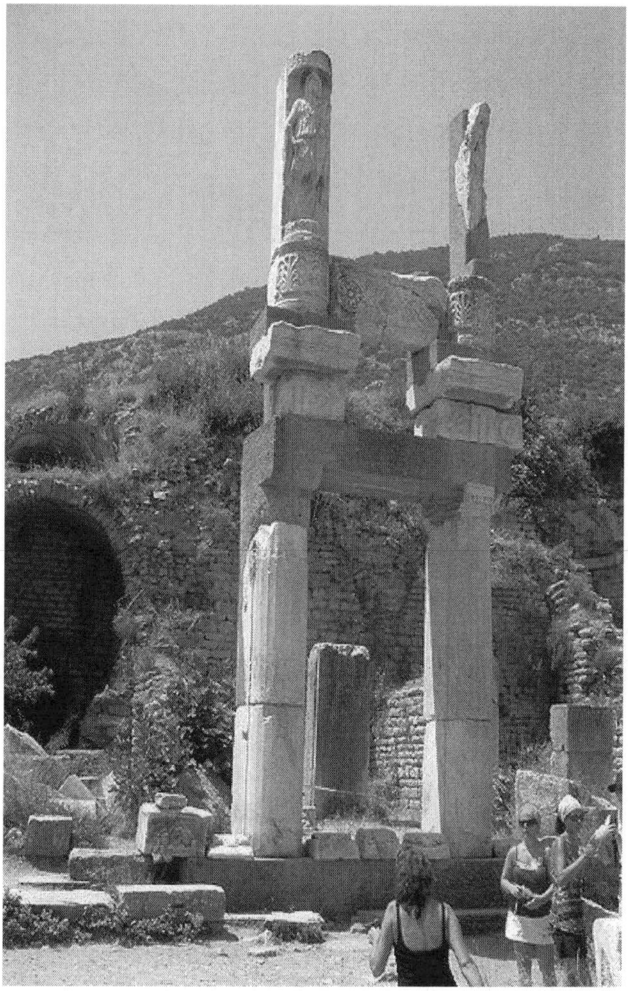

The ruins of Domitian's temple

Domitian was murdered in 96, and his successor, Nerva, ruled for only two years and managed no major accomplishments in Rome or elsewhere. Under Nerva's successor, Trajan (98–117), however, the Roman Empire reached what would be its greatest extent. It was during the reign of Trajan that the Celsus library, another impressive Roman structure in the city of Ephesus, was constructed. The Celsus library was intended to serve as a magnificent memorial for Ptolemaeus, who had served as the chief of staff for building projects in Rome until 92, and the library was positioned so that it faced the morning sun and sat at a 90° angle to the Arch of Mazaeus and Mithridates, by which it was connected to the lower agora. Partitions divided the library's eastern façade into four double columned pavilions, each of which depicted one of the four Virtues: Episteme (Knowledge), Ennoia (Judgment), Arete (Excellence), and Sophia (Wisdom).

The Statue of Wisdom

The Statue of Excellence

The Statue of Judgment

The Statue of Knowledge

The library's interior hall featured three levels of galleries, and a niche located in the rear housed an elaborate marble sarcophagus in which Celsus—a former governor of Asia—himself was interred. A double wall protected the library's scrolls—no less than 10,000 in total—from environmental damage. Finally, the Celsus library contained a number of lecture rooms intended to house visiting sophists, poets, performers, officials, and any other interested citizens.

A statue of Celsus in the library

A picture of the interior of the library

In 117, Trajan was succeeded by his adopted son Hadrian, who had a love for travel, especially to his favorite city Ephesus. Accordingly, Hadrian gave Ephesus permission to construct a second Imperial neokros temple. Hadrian's Temple was constructed by Publius Varius and was likely dedicated to the emperor upon one of his frequent visits to the city between 123 and 128. The small tetrastyle, pro-style temple was located on the southern side of Curates Street. Its entablature was supported by two Corinthian columns and two pillars, the curved Syrian pediment of which depict Tyche (Nike), the goddess of victory, who here was seen wearing a crown decorated with the walls and towers of Ephesus.

Beyond the temple's ornate arch lay its pronaos, which featured an opening for a door. This opening was topped by a tympanum—a semicircular relief that depicted the image of a single female figure (believed to be Medusa) amidst a decorative background of scrolls and acanthus leaves. Through the door was the temple's interior (cella), which had a barrel-vaulted roof.

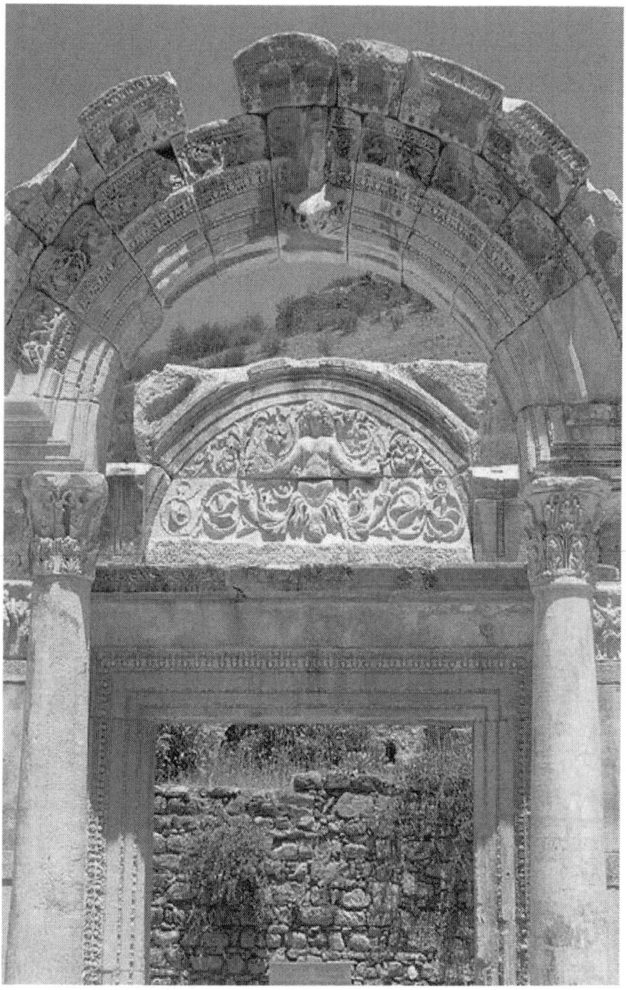

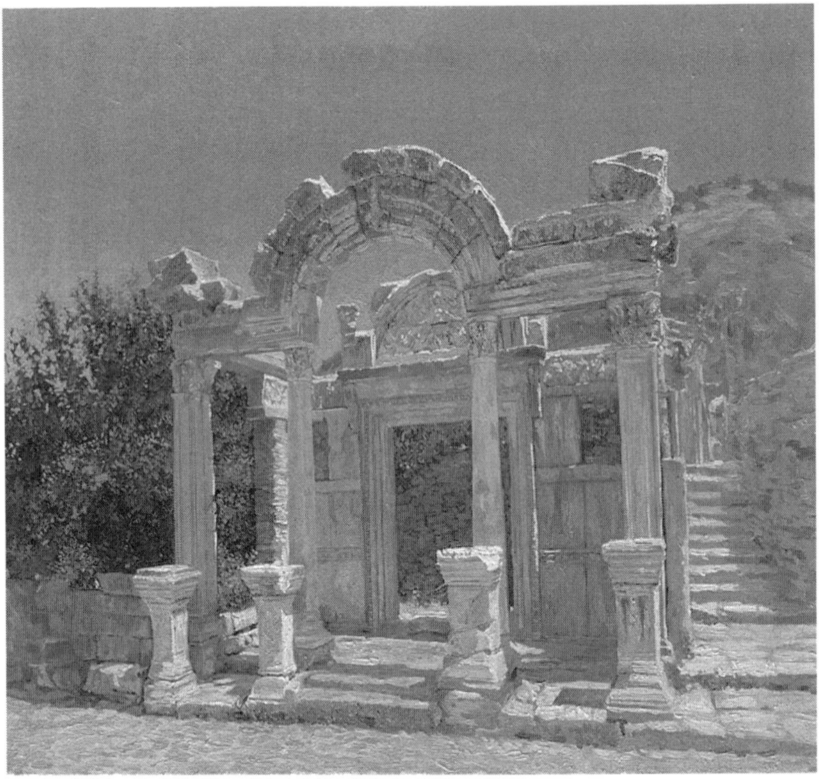

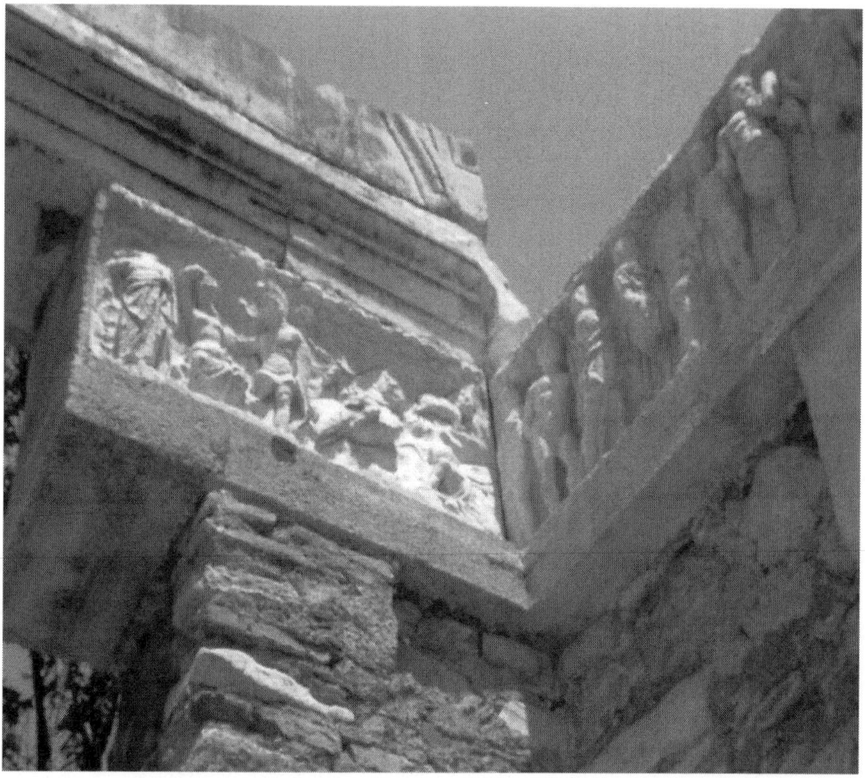

Pictures of Hadrian's Temple

The Ephesians were committed to further enhancing the façade of Hadrian's Temple; long after his death, they continued to erect inscribed pedestals that bore the sculpted images of subsequent emperors, and eventually, the Temple of Hadrian came to contain a spectacular series of friezes. The first slab of the temple's four friezes (one for each side) depicts a male figure—potentially Zeus—a nymph who served to personify the Hypelaios Spring, a warrior, and Androcles, the city's founder, on horseback as he slew the prophesied boar. The second frieze featured the image of a Roman emperor, clad in a military robe and tunic, as he makes a sacrifice in front of a garlanded altar. The hero Theseus stands to the right of this altar and Heracles (from whom four Amazons flee) beside him. According to Greco-Roman mythology, these Amazons took refuge in the Temple of Artemis at Ephesus. The third frieze depicted three more Amazons as they fled from the god Dionysus, who embraced a Satyr in the frieze's center. To his right was Pan, who held a thyrsus, a man on an elephant, and a dancing Maenad holding a cymbal. The fourth frieze depicted a number divinities, including Dea Roma, Selene, Helios, Apollo, Artemis, Heracles, Dionysus, Hermes, Aphrodite, Ares, and Athena. In the midst stood Androcles and his dog.

Chapter 5: Byzantine Ephesus

After Hadrian's death in 138, Ephesus and Roman Asia enjoyed another century of uninterrupted prosperity until it was destroyed by the Goths in 262. After its destruction, the city was never able to recover its former glory, despite some emperors' intermittent attempts at reconstruction in the region.[17] Nevertheless, Ephesus retained some status as the second most important Asian city of the Byzantine Empire and an important center of early Christianity. The apostles and early church fathers often addressed Ephesus in their letters, thus hinting at a strong church presence there.

In the 6th century, the emperor Justinian I (527–565) broke ground on an Ephesian church on the site of what was believed to be the burial place of John the Apostle. The church, which came to be known as the Basilica of St. John, was modeled after the (now lost) Church of the Holy Apostles, which stood in Constantinople. Like most churches of the era, the Basilica of St. John had eight-doorways that opened into its vestibule (narthex). The northern and southernmost of these doors allowed people to access the narthex from outside; three doors to the east opened into the basilica's main hall; the remaining three doors to the west provided access to the outer vestibule (exonarthex). Four short semi-columns belonging to the basilica's upper-level windows stood in the middle part of the narthex. The capitals of these semi-columns were decorated with a distinctively ornate pattern of flora and crosses. The main hall of the church is cruciform with respect to its plan. The western portion of the cross features two aisles and a nave. A wide, single-storied nave stood at the center.

---

[17] Constantine II erected a new public bathhouse, while Arcadius rebuilt the street that led from the harbor to the Great Theater.

Jose Luiz's pictures of the ruins of the Basilica

Above the ground level where the aisles and the nave intersect with the transepts was the basilica's burial areal (bema), and the tomb of Saint John himself was purported to lay below. The decorated columns that surrounded the bema were inscribed with quotations from the Old Testament. An altar stood on the bema's center; the altar's paneled floor featured polychrome geometric decorated panels. Four short columns surrounded the altar, though these were technically part of the ciborium, which accentuated the altar with its four-arched dome. Directly beneath the ciborium were four tombs, the largest of which is believe by some to have belong to Saint John. Early Christians believed that dust taken from this tomb would heal any illness. To the east of the bema, past the transepts, was the basilica's immense semicircular apse, by far its most stunning feature.

The interior of the Basilica of St. John was spectacularly decorated. Mosaics covered the interior of its vault and marble plates adorned its multicolored walls and pillars, perhaps partially thanks to the influence of the Ephesian bishop Hypatius, who was known for enthusiastically advocating the use of images in the church. After construction was completed, the Basilica of St. John was thus covered with the images of saints, a multitude of scenes from both the Old and New Testaments, and a few pieces that could be classified as imperial propaganda, such as Christ crowning the emperor Justinian and paintings clearly reflecting the church as imperially commissioned.

Once finished, the Basilica of St. John almost immediately came to be viewed as one of the most holy churches of its day, but by the 9th century, perhaps due to construction of the Church of John the Theologian, it had fallen into relative obscurity. As it turned out, the city of Ephesus did not long outlast the Basilica of St. John. By the beginning of the Middle Ages, the Ephesian harbor which had so greatly contributed to the city's prominence had finally come to be so silty that it was utterly unusable as a port. Thus, when the Seljuks conquered Ephesus in 1090, their conquest was over nothing more than a small town, and by the 14th century, even this small town was deserted.

Thus, after nearly 3 millennia, the formerly great city once hailed by Pliny the Younger as "the light of Asia" sank into near complete obscurity. It would not truly rise again until 1869, when the site of its Great Temple of Artemis was rediscovered by British archaeologists.

Online Resources

Other books about ancient history by Charles River Editors

Other books about Ancient Greece and Rome on Amazon

Bibliography

Dictionary of Greek and Roman Geography, illustrated by numerous engravings on wood. William Smith, LLD. London. Walton and Maberly, Upper Gower Street and Ivy Lane, Paternoster Row; John Murray, Albemarle Street. 1854.

"Ephesus." Encyclopedia Britannica. 31. Dec. 2014. Web. 9/25/2015.

"Inside the Basilica of St. John." Meander Travel. 2015. Web. 9/25/2015.

Hines, Thomas G. "The Theatre at Ephesus" The Ancient Theatre Archive. 15 Feb. 2009. Web. 9/25/2015

Laale, Hans W. Ephesus (Ephesos): An Abbreviated History from Androclus to Constantine IX. Westbow Press. 2011.

Mark, Joshua J. Ephesos. Ancient History Encyclopedia. 02 Sept. 2009. Web. 9/25/2015.

Printed in Great Britain
by Amazon